Happy Thoughts & Ramblings

Joshua W. McWhorter

ISBN: 0692857818

ISBN-13: 978-0692857816

For Lexi and Brea,

My Happy Thought

CONTENTS

ACKNOWLEDGMENTS

This book was made possible by all the people in my life who believe in and inspire my art. Most of all, those two special ladies who keep this jaded phoenix flying. Lexi and Brea, I love you.

CONCERNING RHYME SCHEME

Does a poem have to rhyme?
Some will tell you, "Yes"

I would like to take the time
To put that notion to the…cucumber

MY HAPPY THOUGHT

I once was greeted by a boy called Pan
He asked me for my happy thought
I told him that the thought was you
He sprinkled dust and off we flew

All the way across the night
To a star the second from the right
This land was plentiful and fair
But woe, my dearests were not there

The Pan perplexed asked, "Why so glum?"
"This is a world of childish fun!"
I lamented, "Pan, my childhood's been had,"
"My life began when they called me Dad"

A dash of dust and off I flew
To bridge the gap from me to you
I soared over snowy mountain peak
And down to the beds where my children sleep

I kissed their sleeping heads but soft
I've missed you my dears…my happy thought

MY MONSTER

Curls upon curls of brunette
And a face that will break a thousand hearts
She is the beautiful monster
Who taught me the meaning of unconditional love

Though not of my blood
She is born of my soul
Like Athena sprung from the mind of Zeus
She is undeniably my daughter

Her intelligence and kindness amaze me daily
Surely she will do great things
Her wit and sarcasm honor me
I pray that she'll never change

She is the apple of my eye
My darling firstborn
First one from my heart
Who can never be torn

I thank daily the divine
That our two souls did pass
A chance meeting
Which became undying love

I didn't have to be her father
But will never regret my choice
For I wouldn't be complete
Without that cherub voice

To the world she is Alexis Somoia McWhorter
To me she is Lexi Monster
And I am and shall always be Daddy
My heart glows!

MY MONKEY GIRL

Flowing blonde locks
And a radiant smile
She is a ray of sunshine
In an increasingly dark world

Her positivity and love
Her bubbly nature
Give me hope for the future
She is a friend to all she meets

Oh, to be so carefree!
With the world as your playground
She jumps and climbs and swings
Like a monkey at play

As I watch her swing through this world
On a vine made of hope and wonder
I can't help but feel
That the world is in good hands

Despite the evil and divisiveness
Of modern society
There are people like her
With the potential to heal old wounds

I am proud every day
To call this one my daughter
She who swings through this world
With a heart overflowing with positivity

It is my dream
That she never change
That she lends her love to this world divided
That she gives all hope as she's given me

To the world she is Brea Fiana McWhorter
To me she is Monkey Girl
And I am and shall always be Daddy
My heart glows!

MY WEALTH

When my time on this earth
Comes to an end
And I look back on my life
My greatest accomplishments
Will always be my children

Dreams made flesh
Their every breath a gift
Their every step a wonder

Though miles apart
We remain one in heart
Parts of a whole indivisible

Fatherhood is wealth in my pocket
The shimmering jewels in my crown
For I have the love of my children
And this heart shall not wear a frown

THE FALL OF TIR NA NOG

Long ago in time of old
Tir na nOg shone bright
The gleaming city of the Fae
A beacon in the night

Good King Manannan sat upon his throne
Surveying all the land
He used his magicks and his might
To see to all demand

All was good in Tir na nOg
Until one fateful day
Good Manannan fell deathly ill
The old king passed away

Not knowing death the Faery folk
They knew not what to do
The king was gone and for the first
Despair began to rule

Tir na nOg began to dim
As King's Magicks began to fade
The fertile lands of Manannan
Were plunged into the shade

That is when the monsters came
The fiendish Imps of dark
They tortured fair and gentle Fae
Tore Tir na nOg apart

There was but one hope for the Fae
Manannan's wee daughter
Alas, her magicks could not halt
These Imps obsessed with slaughter

To protect the tiny queen
And the fate of Tir na nOg
She's sent unto the World of Man
Til time has seen her grow

Trust that she upon return
Will banish darkest night
And Tir na nOg will once again
Be bathed in wondrous light

THE FLAMES OF TIR NA NOG

Tir na nOg was shrouded in flames
As the Imps and Fae fought consumed by rage
This once great city torn asunder
Was set upon by pain and plunder

Far away in World of Man
The young queen's magicks grow
She longs for time when she returns
To dear sweet Tir na nOg

In Tir na nOg the battles raged
One hundred thousand years
Once fine and jolly Faery folk
Reduced to bitter tears

The Faery folk now under foot
A plan the Imps did make
To venture to the World of Man
The Faery Queen to take

A noble Fae rode vigilant
Unto the World of Man
To rescue fragile Faery Queen
From vile Impish hand

Upon arrival Noble Fae
Finds lowly Imps dispatched
Against the Magicks of the Queen
Their evil was outmatched

The time is nigh for her return
Unto the Faery land
Beware to Imps who tarry there
Her vengeance is at hand

THE QUEEN OF TIR NA NOG

The humble Fae of Tir na nOg
Rejoice the queen's return
"Glory be to Good Queen Niamh
For whom so long we've yearned!"

In sorry state was Tir na nOg
Through rape of Impish hand
Springs of plenty all dried up
And scorched infertile land

Niamh did weep to see the sight
Of beloved Faery Home
Entombed in endless night
Where no good seeds are grown

A balm therefore she'd make
She knew just what to do
To save her people so that they
Could shine with light anew

She felt her scheme may weaken her
But chance she had to take
To save the home she loved so dear
The sacrifice she'd make

She shared with the Fae
All her magicks forthright
That with the great power
The Imps they could fight

Take back Tir na nOg
From the fiends at their door
And with the new magicks
The kingdom restore

THE BATTLE FOR TIR NA NOG

Through the Magicks of Niamh
The hopes of the Fae
Are expanded one thousand fold

With this great power
They'd fight back the Imps
And bring back the glories of old

At the gates of the city
They mounted for battle
In armor of mystic design

And there at the center
To lead the assault
Stood the Faery Queen Niamh sublime

Vile and fierce
The Imps did attack
But with Magicks of Old
The Fae held them back

Wave after wave they came
One after one they fell
Despite their numerous vile attacks
They'd not break the Faery spell

The battle raged throughout the night
Fae and Imp fought tooth and nail
They knew that come the morning light
But one side would prevail

As sunlight peeked o'er mountain top
The Imps knew all was lost
Tir na nOg was lost to them
They'd fathom not the cost

Fearful that their time would end
The Imps did beg for mercy
This event in all her wisdom
Good Queen Niamh did not foresee

With magicks great
And wisdom fair
The Imps dark hearts
Niamh did ensnare

Through love and Magicks of the Queen
An avenue to peace was seen
The Imps black hearts were turned to white
They now were Fae enrobed by light

Tir na nOg was saved at last
The queen was on her throne
The noble Fae could now rebuild
Their ancient Faery Home

SKYWARD MAGIC

Aloft upon wings
Yet stable as ground
What magic this is!

Magic of technology
Yet magic nonetheless

Effortless we soar
Above land and cloud
Gods in our Vimana
We make routine a dream of old

We kiss the sky
Make her our lady
She holds us
In her gentle embrace

Roads, rivers, houses, people
They dwell below unaware of us
We peer down and perceive them but faintly
Odd that on ground we too are so small

The sun rises
We greet it as friend
Shining beacon guiding us Eastward
Its light revealing the wonders below

Yes surely tis magic
This thing we call flight
What other could it be?
Come aloft upon Vimana
Surely you'll agree

TESLA'S LAMENT

I envision a world of the future
Where the wonders of science abound
Hatred and hunger are memories
And war is nowhere to be found

I know that this future
I will never see
I hope only that its people
Think fondly of me

I want not for money
I yearn not for fame
To better this world
Is my only aim

There are very many
Who would take this goal from me
Greed, hate, and power
Form the future that they see

Energy crackles around us all
Tis meant for the masses yet held by the small
Small of mind, small of thought, small of caring
Yet large they are of influence

Shall ever these men find broader scope?
Our Mother Earth can only hope
Hope that they do away with their greed
Hope that they help the ones in need

For if the corrupt cannot change their ways
I fear that our world has few numbered days
The future I dream of may not come to pass
And how sad it would be for those living the last

ACROSS THE SEA OF BLACK

I often look out at the stars
And wonder could it be
That somewhere out amongst the stars
There's someone just like me
Staring across the sea of black
Wondering, "Is someone staring back?"

Mathematics say it must be so
Time and space make life discreet
Perhaps some distant future day
Our brothers we shall meet

We'll talk of how in times long past
We looked out at the stars
And dreamed to meet with those who knew
A solitude like ours

The universe may then seem smaller
Once we meet a star-crossed caller
A solace once it's finally known
That we indeed are not alone

BALLAD OF A STAR CHILD

Oh to be among the stars
Far beyond the Earth or Mars
Floating deep into the black
No thought of ever going back

Light of the sun a memory
Too distant for my eyes to see
When quest across the stars is done
Perhaps I'll greet again that sun

But now is time for journey long
To seek the wonders that await
For fire burns within my soul
That only travel can abate

I strap into my vessel proud
Anticipate the coming rush
I feel the force of engines strong
My cheeks begin to flush

I blast through sky and clouds
Far above the sod
I slip the surly bonds of Earth
To touch the face of God

My vessel hurtles faster
Past Jupiter and Saturn
The ship's computer sets the course
It knows the proper pattern

Soon the drivers will engage
I'll pass the speed of light
The Earth in distance will recede
Throughout my space-bound flight

Perhaps in distant day
Another star I'll meet
And round that star a planet
Whose ground shall greet my feet

I long to see that day
First traveler of my kind
As I explore a strange new world
The wonders I will find!

DIVINITY IN A FIREBALL

A ball of gas which floats
So many millions of miles away
Yet its light shines upon us
Its heat warms our day

Its mass is such
That light itself bends unto its will
It has the power to bring forth life
And equally to kill

Hydrogen, Oxygen, Helium coalesce
To form a swirling sphere of gas
A nuclear power plant
Of unfathomable proportion

For eons it burned
Before the Earth was made
And shall burn for eons more
After Earth's final day

To the Egyptians it was Ra
To the Romans, Apollo
Science has named it a star
But is it to us less divine?

Without it we would not be
Particles in space floating free
The Earth we often take for granted
Celestial seed which went unplanted

Perhaps ancient thought was not far askew
From the science of modern time
For they too could see and feel
The benefits of the sunshine

MIND ON A PAGE

Odd thing this brain of mine
Words flow from pen to page
Yet by tongue and mouth
They twist

What frustration!
To so keenly speak
By way of written art
Yet struggle at conversation

I wonder if I seem aloof
Not speaking when I ought
Among the other plebs
Who so freely word their thought

Let me assure you now
That is not my intent
Would that I knew how
My voice would join the bent

Perhaps my odd condition
Causes friends and loves to flee
Could be that if I could converse
Then more would stand by me

Tis lonely in my tortured mind
So many words fight to escape
My mouth does keep them prisoner
So they escape onto the page

Once on the page
I'm free to speak
These words my mouth had lost
And worry not the consequence

Perhaps that is the key
Through art all can be said
That when in conversation
Is better left in head

MEDIA

You've forgotten your duty
As fourth estate
And devolved to a business
Of slinging hate

There's but one side
You're meant to take
That is the side of truth

You're tasked with the burden
Of presenting the facts
But facts must be backed by proof

Your job is not to tell us
What you think we want to hear
To hold us close and softly
Whisper nothings in our ear

Give us the facts
And let us decide
Don't attempt to influence
The picking of a side

Stop breeding division
With partisan fluff
We don't have the time
For that childish stuff

A STATE OF DISUNION

They each play a side
But they're in the same boat
If you show them a stone
They will claim it can float

Liars and thieves
That's the name of the game
It's enough it could drive
The wisest insane

When did it all go so horribly skewed?
How did our system wind up so unglued?
Some will insist that it's moral decay
But what if our nation was always this way?

Founded by slavers touting "Liberty for All"
Who denied said liberty when the masses came to call
Saved by a man who'd've freed no slave if he could
Just so long as the union stood

From the start we've been a nation conflicted
Lofty goals subjected by actions constricted
Freedom is great to talk about
But has it truly come about?

The flinging of shit seems the rule of the land
But who does it hit when it flies through the fan?
Certainly not the ones at the top
When will this travesty come to a stop?

I believe that this land can be great as we dream
But whether it will still remains to be seen
We need people invested to put in the work
Enough with this popular circle-jerk

MEA CULPA, SARCASTICALLY

I am the aggressor
The oppressor
The one you should fear

I work for nothing
And am given everything
Privilege is the life
Into which I was born

I am strong
And you are weak
It is up to you
To take what I have been given

Take this privilege
Make it your own
Subjugate me as I deserve
Make the world over in your image

I am but a man
A spectre of hate
A hostile avatar
Of THE PATRIARCHY

Take this world
Bend it to your will
Make it your own
I'm sure you'll do swimmingly

EGALITARIAN

Your color of skin
Makes no difference to me
Your demeanor and actions
Form the person I see

Your gender does not determine
Your level of worth
Each person's needs
Are a right of their birth

Opportunity should come to all those who seek it
We should all have a chance to stand tall and speak
And to lend strength and voice
To ones made to feel weak

Are we all different?
Well sure, but we're all part of this game
In at least one respect
We are all quite the same

We are all human
And that has to count for something

THOUGHTS ON THOUGHTLESSNESS

So I'm officially divorced
Back on the market as they say
In a business I didn't ask to get back into
And in which I had little stock when half my age

Dating is different at 30
In this increasingly fast-paced world
Online? Offline? Both conundrums
Where to start?

Odd that things which ought to be thought through
Are thoughtless in our youth
Animal instinct sparked by hormonal urge
If only things were still so easy

Or perhaps it is yet so simple
But with age, stupid things like intellect
Get in the way of what we want
We think too much on what should be thoughtless

Might that be why marriages fail?
We think too much on what is wrong
Forget to be happy
With what is right

My situation at present is not ideal
But I have hope it will improve
The wounds of my past will one day heal
I can be happy with that

THE HEART'S FOREVER

Is forever relative?
Physics tells us yes

Time and space are one
Fluid, malleable
They ebb and flow
To the whim of gravity and mass

The human heart is linear
It is gifted but so many beats over the course of a life
And then time for the heart comes to an end
But time for the hearts left behind marches on

The heart therefore in its time
Can beat the laws of physics
The heart creates a forever
All its own

Gravity cannot bend the heart
To make its time expand
It has but few beats in its time
Until it meets its end

Enjoy your forever in the time that you have
For the heart's forever is love

JADED PHOENIX

At the age of thirty
His life starts anew
From the ashes of dreams
Torn asunder

Hesitant he starts
Down a new path
With eyes and heart
Full of wonder

Unsure of his future
Jaded by his past
He hopes for a dream
He may never achieve

This year has brought changes
Things he struggled to perceive
But through all his strife
He'd still like to believe

The struggle will lessen
He'll strive through the pain
Pick up the pieces
Come out of it sane

His fresh start will be a blessing
A chance at happiness
With someone who'll respect him
Unique soul that he is

He knows not where she is
Or when or where they'll meet
But when he finds her he will know
His heart's again complete

Jaded though he is
He hopes for better times
Walking hand in hand with one
Who makes this life sublime

DEPARTED MUSE

A muse long departed
Yet still on my mind
She brought clarity
And order to thought

Wondrous colors
And word she did bring
By her influence
Great art was wrought

In times with her
How quickly words flew
From mind through hand
To pen

No barrier was there
Twixt ethereal plane
And this lowly realm
Of men

But gone now is my muse
First name Mary
Last name Jane
Initials THC

I sit and ponder
As I write
When will you
Come back to me?

SECOND-HAND JAZZ

Sitting in this lobby
Hours on end
The sounds of second-hand jazz
Make me want to take drill to head

Steel bit through frontal lobe
Messy and painful
Homemade lobotomy
Perhaps that may halt this noise

Would that I knew
From whence this infernal cacophony'd sprung
I'd smash dread machine
And the torture'd be done

But alas! I know not
From whence decibels quake
So perhaps then
My own precious hearing I'll take

Needles!
Yes needles I'll take
To the drums of my ear
And then no more second-hand jazz will I hear

What is that you say?
I'm afraid I don't know
Since I must read your lips
You will have to talk slow!

ACCEPTANCE OF THE BIFURCATED SOUL

Soy el Diablo Blanco del Valle
A fish out of water in two worlds
Too white to be brown
And too brown to be white

I don't speak Spanish
But I can pronounce it perfectly
Despite lack of Hispanic blood
I can cook like una abuelita

Growing up white on the border
Is an exercise in isolation
Despite the acceptance of friends
You are never the same as everyone else

I am a creature
Of bifurcated soul
Disparate halves
Form an amalgamated whole

With the brown I am comfortable
But will never belong
With the white I belong
But will never feel comfortable

They call me "Honorary Mexican"
Accept me as a brother
But can I accept myself?
Embrace my nature as the other?

Perhaps the problem is this
I'm not that different at all
If my brothers are in need of help
Would I not answer the call?

Division is made in the mind
Understanding bred in the soul
Through the acceptance of my brothers
I became part of a whole

Not wholly white
Not wholly brown
The best of both
Todo RGV

A BENEFICIAL OIL SPILL

Tis hard for those
Who are truly loyal
In a sea of deceit
A small drop of oil

Surrounded yet alone
This is the experience of the loyal
Part of the world yet apart
From the multitude seeking to manipulate

The corrupt many surround
They try to mix
But the loyal are steadfast
They hold strong to their conviction

Due to numbers the manipulative sea
Think themselves the strong
They surround, envelope
Feel free to work their wrong

But when a loyal one
Is met by many more
That single drop of oil grows
Emboldened by the score

This oil slick of loyalty
Will push aside deceit
Separate the waters
As more loyal ones they meet

How funny that an oil spill
Be equated with something good
But if analogy fits
I'm confident it should

NOT GUILTY

I reject the narrow-minded notion
Of white guilt
I vehemently refuse to take responsibility
For things which happened long before my birth

I have enslave no one
I hold ill will for no man
And I judge not
On the basis of race

Do I deny that racism exists?
Of course I do not
But I refuse to apologize
For the racism of others

Some will insist that prejudice
Is inherent in my race
That I should be sorry
For my color of face

This is a fallacy
The sins of the past
Have no bearing on me
I shall be judged by my actions

MILLENNIAL

My generation is weak
We need trigger warnings
And safe spaces
Our feelings have replaced logic

From birth we have been fed lies
Told that masculinity is toxic
And feminism is equality
Gilded in the name of progress

We are a generation repressed
We live in the here and now
We whine about problems
Yet take no responsibility

My generation is a sheltered one
Living in a bubble of protection
When the bubble bursts
Chaos ensues

Contrarian is my generation
Preaching tolerance for all
Yet when faced with differing opinion
The claws come out

We believe ourselves infallible
Too easily do we take offense
True tolerance is lost on us
As well as common sense

I fear for my generation
And the world that we'll soon run
I don't at this point see us
Making it better for anyone

BUTTHURT NATION

I don't like you
So you're a fascist
I don't agree with you
So watch the buzz words fly!

Racist, sexist, misogynist!
Bet I can name more than you!
The ambiguous, interfaith, secular lord said,
"Let insert preferred pronoun
Who is the most offended cast the first stone"

As I draw back to throw
I am pelted by ten stones
Ten fools who believe themselves
More oppressed than I

This is highly problematic
A clear sign of intolerance
My feelings are vitally important
And you need to agree with them!

Where is my safe space?
Where can I hide?
I can't deal with this
Somebody save me!!

AN ARCHER OUT OF PRACTICE

Cupid notches his arrow
Draws back
Lets fly the missile
And in the dirt it falls

The promise of a shared happiness
Collapsed to dust
Blown to the winds
And scattered

Weeps he, the cherub
At the failure of his charge
To miss his mark
The folly of an archer out of practice

For the work of Cupid
Of late is light
Little use for truest love
In a world self-obsessed

Truly, though his aim be sound
Flee from his arrow do many
Though plentiful benefit come from his shot
They often want of it not any

So flies he back to Olympus
To sit upon a cloud
And dream of days long past
When romance gripped the crowd

In his dream they cheer him
As he lets his arrows fly
Magical streaks of gleaming red
Which fill the bluest sky

Each missile hits its mark
A successful mission mastered
The cherub is lauded with praise
And sincerely he is thanked

Vain is he not in his acceptance
His work is vital and fair
For without the love he spreads
The people would begin not to care

What a world would it be without caring?
The dream cherub wonders aloud
Caring is the current
Upon which love arrows fly

Awakes he in horror
As he stares at the sky
He queries himself
Perhaps the careless is I?

Though run they from my arrow
Velocity and aim are burden mine
I must care
To hit my mark

Emboldened sets he out
With care to practice aim
That someday may he make
His dreams and life the same

THE VOID

Upon a time I kissed your face
Praised the day I set eyes upon it
Yet now I'd rather spit in said face
And rue the day it next darkens my eye

Odd how feelings change
How dearest love
Can so steadily deteriorate
To purest loathing

The face that once I dreamt
To never live without
Belongs to the person
Who tore my world apart

Be this the destiny of love?
That one you trust most
Be the one to destroy you
Why then trust at all?

But surely trust we must
And brave the possible pain
For braving what may pain us
Can help to keep us sane

I can say I do not miss you
Wish not to have you back
I do sincerely thank you
For the lessons you have taught

For now I know
The type of woman to avoid
No longer will I compromise
Just to fill this void

POST TENEBRAS LUX

Your speech is protected
Rejoice in that
Let no one take it from you
Post tenebras lux

Your individuality is a gift
It makes you who you are
Let no one put you in a box
Post tenebras lux

Your opinions are your right
When they attack you in the street
Crying, "This is what democracy looks like!"
Post tenebras lux

People will disagree
As well they should
The best progress comes through discord
Post tenebras lux

Darkness will fall
The struggle will be faced
And then will come the light
Post tenebras lux my friends

TWIGS AND PEBBLES

Sticks and stones
May break my bones
But words
Will never hurt me

A lesson from childhood
Often discarded
As feelings usurp
Logic and reason

Words are wondrous things
They hold tremendous power
A word in the right mouth
Can turn a thousand ears

Despite their power and influence
Words are incapable of violence
They have no arms with which to punch
No teeth with which to bite

Words are simply tools
They are used for good
They are used for evil
But are by nature neutral

I implore you to fear no word
Nor others' chosen use
Difference of opinion
Is not tantamount to abuse

We learned this lesson
In childhood
It would do well
To not forget

Sticks and stones
May break my bones
But words
Will never hurt me

BEACON

Nationalism does not
A Nazi make
Pride and love of country
Need not set faint hearts aquake

There are no brown-shirt monsters
To pound upon your door
No jackboot wearing tyrants
Out to euthanize the poor

It is no sin to love your country
To want for it the best
To wave it as a beacon
An example for the rest

I feel that we have lost this
In our fear to make offense
Our worry for what the world will think
Makes the situation tense

Nationalism is not a dirty word
Just one misunderstood
An old friend with reacquaintance
Might do this world some good

So love your nation
Make it great
Be a beacon for the world
Stand together in the light
Red, white, and blue unfurled

Those huddled masses shall see
And be emboldened by the sight
Soon enough they too will strive
To join you in the light

HEARTS AND MINDS

Long ago in time of myth
An epic war did rage
A fierce battle fought
For the soul of a world

A war this was
Between two kings
Amoros of Cardia
And Logikos of Cerebras

Amoros ruled his land
With the fire of passion
To heed his people's feelings
Was his chosen fashion

Logikos on other hand
Did govern from the mind
Reason and careful planning
Had no one left behind

For many years the people of Cardia
Were content to be given their wants
A happiness achieved
Through excess

Upon a time however
The surpluses did run short
Amoros no longer could freely give
Such great benefit to his court

The people of Cardia turned eye to the North
To the plentiful land of Cerebras
They asked of Amoros,
"What can be done to bring such glory back to us?"

Amoros resolved to attack
His neighbor to the North
Sure his steadfast passions
Would bring a conquest forth

Thus the war began
And raged for many year
Cerebras would defend with strategy
Cardia would attack with fear

Back and forth the battles raged
Amoros advancing with passion
And Logikos countering with thought
A constant stalemate

Both lands beset by war
Suffered as never before
A solution had to be found
A way to turn their fates around

So a meeting there was set
Between the two great kings
To end the bitter war
Move on to better things

Upon their conference
Logikos reasoned cooperation was a must
Likewise Amoros felt in his heart
Twas for the better of all to trust

Therefore a truce was made
That they'd work toward the best
Cardia and Cerebras would work in tandem
To better face any test

And so it's been since those old days
When two kings joined as one
Cerebras and Cardia
Together in the sun

HOMINID CRUSTACEAN

A pox upon my deficient melanin!
Oh! To walk long in the sun
Without shortly resembling
Something akin to a human lobster!

What hassle it is!
To slather oneself
With creams whiter
Than own ivory complexion!

How futile as well!
For without reapplication
And constantly seeking shade
The burns will still surely come!

What genius!
The ancestors long past
Leaving native lands
For the scorching sun of Texas!

DOUBLE SHIFT

The head droops
The eyes heavy

Working sixteen hours
Awake for twenty-four

The poet's mind exhausted
The hand refused to write

Walking the razor edge of delirium
I'm off to bed, good night!

ABOUT THE AUTHOR

Joshua W. McWhorter was born 75 million years ago in the Galactic Confederation of Lord Xenu. He came to Earth via time-space displacement circa 1986 in an effort to corrupt the weakling minds of humanity. In an unfortunate twist of circumstance, his devious mind was separated from his body and forced to take refuge in the form of a pitiful human infant. As a result he had no choice but to live amongst and as one of them until the day he might ultimately enact his plot. His interests include genetic manipulation, programmable memory implants, and the chemical composition of salt water taffy. He enjoys long walks on the beach, puppies, and the collected works of the visionary film director John Hughes. He spent his earthbound adolescence in the Rio Grande Valley where he succeeded in vanquishing the notorious Chupacabra. He currently resides in Garland, TX where he plots his impending revenge against the inescapable feminine wiles of Jessica Rabbit.